7/16/06

To: Katie
I saw this book
and thought of you!
You are my best friend and
Will miss you much.
Have fun in FL!
Love you lots,
Beth Howard

# Ireland

## A Photographic Journey

# Ireland

## A Photographic Journey

Emma Howard

Photographs by David Lyons

BARNES
& NOBLE

NEW YORK

This edition published by Barnes & Noble, Inc., by arrangement with Compendium Publishing Limited

2006 Barnes & Noble Books

M 10 9 8 7 6 5 4 3 2 1

ISBN 0 7607 7336 X

Editor: Don Gulbrandsen
Design: Danny Gillespie/Compendium Design

Printed in China through Printworks Int. Ltd.

**PAGE 1:** Fuchsia are so common by the roadside in Ireland they could almost be the national flower.

**PAGES 2–3:** Landscape in the Sperrin Mountains across the Glenelly River Valley to Sawel Mountain, Co. Tyrone.

**RIGHT:** Tory Island.

# Contents

# Introduction

Ireland's long and diverse history is obvious to any-body who travels through it. Indeed, Ireland is a land that wears its history on its sleeve, clearly visible to those who wish to discover it. There are many mega-lithic sites scattered all across the country that show its importance in Neolithic times. The Celtic crosses and ruins of monasteries attest to the arrival of Christianity—and later to the rampages of the Vikings. There are other reminders of harsh times—of domination in the form of ruined castles and strongholds across the country that hark back to times of war and invasion. There are also many unique sites, such as the hill of Tara in County Meath, which was a pivotal symbol of the Irish kingship. This book attempts to provide a flavor of the Irish history that is still visible today through the lens of the Irish photographer David Lyons, whose skill with a camera shines out of every photograph.

**Earliest Times**

Very little is known about prehistoric Ireland, although historians are now moderately confident that settlers had reached the country by 8000 B.C. These early settlers would have been hunters and fish-ermen living off the land. In fact the first evidence of humans are round houses discovered at Mount Sandel. They are made from branches covered with sod and date from around this period. They were built by what is described as a small number of pork and salmon-eating people. Neolithic times (from about 4000 B.C.) saw a change in farming tech-niques—along with cattle that were brought across the sea by new settlers—that enabled farmers to cul-tivate in one place and remain there. No longer did hunter-gatherers have to move across the country in search of food. With agriculture came settlements and social life.

At around this time the first dolmens (large stone tombs) were erected. These megalithic structures show some sophistication in the culture of the times, especially because some are very intricate. For example, the tomb at Creevykeel in County Sligo has an open-air oval forecourt in front of its entrance, and the famous passage tomb at Newgrange in County Meath was built so that on the shortest day of the year, the winter solstice (December 21), the rays of the sun shine gradually along the rising passageway and finally blaze all the way into the central burial chamber.

Bronze Age Ireland, which began around 2000 B.C., produced many artifacts of interest to historians. Dublin's National Museum houses distinctive pottery, swords, and shields. During this period it is thought that Ireland became one of the principal suppliers of gold and copper, shipping both raw materials and finished products to Britain and Europe. The Bronze Age is also apparent in the appearance of stone circles the most significant are found around Cork, Kerry, and Ulster. Surprisingly, these monuments seem to have been used as primitive observatories.

When considering early Ireland most people think of the Celts. The romantic notion that they swept into Ireland and made it their own is far from the truth. The so-called "founding fathers" of Ireland were little more than a gang of well-armed bullies with grand ambitions. Their "taking" of Ireland from the original settlers would have involved very little effort because the population at that time was so small there was little chance of any strong opposition. In truth, it is more likely that the Celtic colonization took place over many years, with the two cultures melding together, rather than one completely usurping the other. An example of this merging is evident in the language of the country; although there are slight touches of pre-Celtic languages, the established language became Irish-Gaelic which is a unique form of Celtic with localized touches.

Although it is debatable whether the Romans invaded Ireland, their influence did make it across the sea even if their armies did not. There was a great wine trade and several Roman artifacts have been discovered dating from as early as the first century A.D.

**BELOW:** Farmland south of Tullow looking toward Mount Leinster, Co. Carlow.

Perhaps taking inspiration from the intrepid Roman conquerors, the Irish populace decided to conquer new lands of their own, starting with Britain. They established very successful settlements in Scotland, so successful that the original language of the Picts was replaced by that of the Irish. Even the word "Scotland" comes from the name of the Irish (or Scoti) who settled themselves there. There was also a significant Irish settlement in the west of Wales. To the north in Anglesey, Denbighshire, and Caernarvonshire, colonists from Leinster reigned, even giving their name to the Lleyn peninsula in Gwynedd (from the Laigin dynasty).

### The Arrival of Christianity

Considering their proximity to each other and all the interaction between the two countries, it was not long before the religion of Britain found its way to Irish shores. At that time the predominant religion was Christianity. In fact one of Ireland's most celebrated saints—Patrick, who lived in the fifth century—was British. Having been kidnapped as a young boy and taken to Ireland as a slave, he spent much of his life there and became a devout Christian. Even after his subsequent escape from slavery and return to England, he never forgot his Irish and his "lost" compatriots. He soon returned to the place of his original incarceration with the intention of spreading the word of God. Although he is often credited with converting the whole of Ireland to Christianity, this is highly unlikely. It is far more probable that Christianity had begun to spread slowly across the country many years before Patrick's return. There were certainly other missionaries in Ireland at the time, yet their exploits have not received the fame—or the annual celebratory day of drinking that modern times have made St. Patrick's Day—of their more famous counterpart. Whoever is

responsible, Ireland did embrace Christianity and in particular, monasticism. Many monasteries were built during the sixth century A.D. Great monasteries like those in Kildare or Cork became centers of the religious community, enjoying wealth, influence, and connections with the powerful and rich.

The church's effect on the burgeoning society of Ireland at the time was vital. Latin was studied under church instruction starting at the end of the sixth century. During the next two centuries the church was instrumental in writing down and compiling laws dealing with social issues, theft, the idea of sanctuary inside the House of God, and the "law of the innocent" that gives women and children protection in times of war. Perhaps one of the most influential and contentious issues addressed by the church at this time was that of the divinely ordained monarch. It was a matter that was beneficial to the church and a potential pitfall to any aspiring future king. Rival kings would only be victorious with the sanction of the church and the church would only sanction those hopefuls it deemed expedient to its cause—whatever that may be.

Despite this, the medieval kings of Ireland were still a force to be reckoned with, although much is still uncertain about what exactly "kingship" meant during the middle ages. It is clear that there were different levels of ruler, each one more powerful than the next—a kind of ladder of royalty, so to speak. This started with the ri tuaithe, who was the ruler of a local kingdom; next came the "middle management," the ruiri, who presided over a number of local kings; then finally, the ri ruirech, the provincial king, who had substantial power. It is unclear, however, if there was at this time a high king (ard-ri). It would seem that the UiNeill clan came close to absolute rule in Ireland but did not quite achieve it. The constant

## OLIVER CROMWELL

Oliver Cromwell (1599–1658) landed in Ireland with 3,000 battle-ready troops in 1649. The civil war in England was over and Cromwell's mind was set on crushing the rebellion by Roman Catholics who held most of Ireland at that time. Following the massacre of English and Scottish settlers in Ireland, his intent was to quell and terrorize all rebels and any remaining royalists. He marched through Ireland, slaughtering garrisons and civilians without distinction. When rebelling garrisons surrendered, it was normal practice for Cromwell to slaughter all soldiers without guilt. Cromwell's campaign finally ended at Clonmel. After a fierce battle the defenders secretly withdrew under the cover of night, leaving Cromwell's troops to claim victory. Although his stay in Ireland was relatively short—he left in May 1650— the ramifications of his campaign were far-reaching. Catholics across the country had their land stripped away from them. Some were given the option of taking less-fertile land in Connacht; an unfortunate few were even shipped to the West Indies as slaves. Cromwell's reputation for brutality was infamous. A popular Irish oath at the time was "The Curse of Cromwell on you!"

warring and fierce competition among all the clans—and indeed, violent disputes between members of the clans themselves—meant no single ruler could come to power for any length of time, unless there was a strong stimulus such as a common enemy to fight.

### The Vikings

Ireland's inhabitants soon had that common enemy—the Vikings. In A.D. 795 a Viking raiding party attacked the east coast at Rathlin on Lambay Island and another site—Iona—almost destroying the monasteries based there. The monastery at Iona would endure another Viking attack in A.D. 806 that saw the slaughter of most of its brethren. Deciding it would be safer on the mainland, the survivors moved to Kells in County Meath and built a new monastery there.

Obviously the monks were in no position to fend off marauders and put up little resistance to them. The Vikings had no sense of the ground being sacred or a place of sanctuary—they just knew that these monasteries were a source of great wealth. For almost 30 years the entire Irish coast was bombarded by Viking attacks. The assaults remained fairly random until the A.D. 830s when the first significant inland raids started to occur. By A.D.837 large Scandinavian fleets sailed down the rivers Liffey and Boyne, and by 840 Viking settlements had begun—allowing them to remain in Ireland during the winter.

As the Vikings spent more and more time settled in Ireland, the relationship between the two peoples shifted. The raiders had inflicted many horrors on the inhabitants of the country, but there were also positive influences that emerged. Dublin was the first settlement for the Vikings and it was to become a very important one. Ports in Dublin grew larger as the maritime trade increased; the first coins were minted; knowledge of boat building was shared; and there was an introduction of new art styles. Yet despite all this, the violence was never forgotten, especially by the local Irish kings. Perhaps learning from their Scandinavian invaders, Gaelic kings started using the ruthless Viking ways to settle any disputes. Battles were fought mercilessly and the strongest king would declare himself high king of all Ireland. It was one such high king, Brian Boru of the Dal Chais, who began serious opposition to the Norse. He vanquished Mealsechaill II, King of Tara (who had formed alliances with the Vikings to expedite his rise to power), and marched on Dublin the following year. Once in power he tried to undo some of the damage that the Vikings had done to his country with the restoration of religion, education, and culture. After his death at the battle of Clontarf, the next century was punctuated with scuffles between local kings for Brian's seat of power and this disarray paved the way for the arrival of the Normans in 1169.

LEFT: Detail of pillar top at Boyle Abbey, Co. Roscommon.

BELOW LEFT: Landscape near Jamestown, Co. Roscommon.

### DANIEL O'CONNELL

Born in County Kerry in 1775, O'Connell (1775–1847) earned himself the nickname "The Liberator" for his pioneering efforts in emancipating the Catholics. He was educated abroad and came home to Ireland to become a lawyer. Being a Catholic he was in an ideal position not only to experience, but also to fight against, the adversities and injustices facing Catholics during the nineteenth century. He founded the Catholic Association in 1823, which campaigned for equal rights for Catholics. A charming and charismatic man with impressive speaking skills, he was elected Member of Parliament for County Clare in 1828 but, because he was a Catholic, he was not allowed to take his office. The next year witnessed the Catholic Emancipation Act, which allowed Catholics to hold seats in Parliament and to take jobs in public office. He also founded the Repeal Association in 1840 and began a series of "Monster Meetings" in an attempt to overwhelm the government by sheer numbers. These meeting were hugely popular and raised Nationalist sentiment to boiling point. Worried, the government sent out the troops to stop the largest meeting planned for October 8, 1843, in Clontarf. O'Connell cancelled the meeting—concerned for his followers—and soon after the Repeal Association collapsed. Four years later, O'Connell himself was dead.

## JAMES CONNOLLY

Born into poverty in 1868 in Edinburgh and working by the age of ten, it is not surprising that this self-educated, talented orator so readily adopted the ethos of Marxism. Throughout his life Connolly (1868–1916) fought for socialism with a dogged determination and single-mindedness. He planned successful strikes throughout Ireland including the famous Belfast textile workers' strike of 1911. In response to his well-planned strikes, Connolly suffered the Dublin lockouts of 1913 where management tried, unsuccessfully, to crush the mounting rebellion. With the onset of World War I, Connolly's concerns regarding Irish freedom were amplified. The idea of conscription in Ireland was a major worry because it would hamper the revolution he so desperately wanted. On Easter Monday 1916 Connolly and other Republican leaders, including Patrick Pearse and Bulmer Hobson, led the way for what was supposed to be a widespread insurrection. This was not the case. The revolution was mainly confined to the Dublin area and lasted less than a week before being crushed by the authorities. The leaders were captured by the British army and subjected to a mockery of a trial. Naturally all were found guilty and sentenced to death. The savagery of Connolly's death has made him a larger than life martyr for the cause of Irish freedom. Wounded and unable to stand, James Connolly was executed by a firing squad while strapped to a chair.

RIGHT: Carrowmore prehistoric megalithic cemetery, Co. Sligo. In the background, on top of Knockaree mountain, Queen Maeve's Grave—a huge cairn—can be seen.

## The Normans

The death of Brian Boru left a power vacuum that was soon filled by Turloch Mor O'Conor—and when he died his son, Rory, took on the mantle of high king. To take his place as ruler he ousted Dermot Mac Murrough, King of Leinster, who had seized the Leinster seat at the time of Turloch's death. Dermot had made many enemies in Ireland by seizing the throne from someone who was viewed to be the rightful heir, and he expected little assistance from the local kings in taking back his throne. Instead he fled to England to beseech the help of King Henry II, and promised his allegiance in return for the throne of Ireland. Although Henry did not offer his armies directly, he gave Dermot permission to seek help from the nobles of England. One such nobleman was Richard FitzGilbert de Clare, an Anglo-Norman known as Strongbow. In return for his help, Strongbow would be married to Dermot's daughter, Aoife, and was promised the throne of Leinster upon Dermot's death. Returning to Ireland with his new allies, Dermot soon defeated Rory's forces and before long Dublin had been captured. There Dermot was recrowned King of Leinster. Once this had been accomplished, Dermot announced his plan to make himself high king but died shortly after in 1171. At this point Strongbow, bolstered by support from those still faithful to Dermot and his superior military powers, made his claim on the throne of Leinster.

At this point King Henry became concerned. Naturally the last thing he wanted was the evolution of an independent kingdom next door to his own. So to keep Strongbow in check, he made an immediate visit to Ireland. While there he confirmed Strongbow's entitlement to the throne of Leinster and named him fief to the crown of England, but at the same time claimed all the major seaports, including Dublin, as his own. However, Henry's intent was not limited to keeping his nobles in check, he wanted to pave the way for his son, John, to become ruler of Ireland and also heal the relationship between himself and the church. (Things had become strained since the murder of Archbishop Thomas Becket in 1170.) Henry had received an endorsement from the pope many years previously, which stated he had the right to rule Ireland as king but he had never been in a position to enforce it—until now. Henry thought that if the pope could witness him making efforts to promote the church in Ireland, then the relationship would heal.

He was right. In 1172 Pope Alexander III officially sanctioned his right to rule in Ireland. With this papal approval the Irish kings eventually all came forward to submit themselves to Henry. He, in return, had to respect these Irish kings and guarantee them protection from attack. Unfortunately he did

not keep his promise and the Irish rulers had their first taste of English politics. On leaving Ireland in 1172, Henry appointed Hugh de Lacy as his representative in Ireland and awarded him the entire county and former kingdom of Meath. Obviously the existing Irish King of Meath was overlooked by the English ruler. Henry's deceitful example was quickly copied by the many Norman barons who began flooding into Ireland shortly after his departure. Estates were seized and great tracts of land taken until almost three quarters of Ireland was under Norman occupation. The fact that he had not yet conquered the whole of Ireland was not lost on Henry and in a bid to make the royal hold on the country complete, he signed the Treaty of Windsor in 1175 with Rory O'Conor. In exchange for O'Conor's loyalty to the English throne, Henry would grant him all the lands that had not and could not be conquered—a pattern of "English land" and "Irish land" had begun to form.

## Feudal Ireland

In 1177 Henry made his son "Lord of Ireland," further cementing the Norman although complete control was still beyond his grasp. The continued presence of the Normans had a significant effect on Irish culture. For example, they introduced a feudal land-holding system to the island in which the King owned all the land but granted it to the aristocracy in exchange for money or loyalty. They, in turn, divided the land to lesser nobles who, in turn, rented it out to tenants.

This feudal system was also apparent in the politics of the time. The administrator was in control of military and civil organizations, but had help from knowledgeable officials in councils. At the end of the thirteenth century these councils were being referred to as parliament—the Normans had laid down the foundations for a practical working government.

Ireland under the Normans grew and new towns, such as Athlone and Kilkenny, developed. Linguistic change was also a consequence of the occupation. English became the spoken language of the island. Stone castles began to appear across the country, because the occupying Normans wanted to strengthen their defenses. The established Norman castle design featured a central keep surrounded by walls; those that have survived today are still imposing, a good example being Carrickfergus Castle in County Antrim.

## Edward Bruce

Despite having such a huge influence over Ireland the Anglo-Norman rulers had yet to consolidate complete control and were constantly distracted by influential and stubborn local Irish kings. They also had to contend with other aggressive colonial hopefuls. In

**BELOW: Looking northeast over Lough Mask, Co. Mayo.**

1315 Edward Bruce invaded Ireland. This was in direct response to England's attempts to conquer Scotland. King Edward I—the "Hammer of the Scots"—had made considerable inroads into Wales and then had turned his attentions northward. He defeated William "Braveheart" Wallace at Falkirk in 1298 but the stubborn Scots withstood him. He died marching north again in 1307 and was succeeded by his son, Edward II. Robert Bruce, crowned king of Scotland in 1306, was a powerful figure and a strong adversary. Robert concluded that much of Edward's manpower and resources had been withdrawn from Ireland to bolster his attack on Scotland, leaving the island open to assault. Not only would this loosen the English hold on Ireland, but might provide Robert Bruce's brother, Edward, with a kingdom all his own. After allying themselves with Irish leaders and defeating the Norman Richard de Burgo in battle, Edward Bruce was crowned king of Ireland in 1316. His rule was short-lived, however; he was killed in battle in 1318 and the crown reverted once more to Anglo-Norman hands. Edward's adventure had, however, proved that English rule was vulnerable.

### The Statutes of Kilkenny

As time went on, the Norman nobles showed their willingness to ally themselves with Gaelic leaders, destabilizing the power of the English king. As a result Edward III sent his son, Lionel, to Ireland as the "king's lieutenant." He initiated the Statutes of Kilkenny, a radical way of trying to keep the "Englishness" of the settlers untainted. They ruled that there should be no trading with the Gaelic inhabitants and there should be absolutely no inter-marriage or intimate relations of any kind. Irish music and poetry were forbidden (just in case it muddy the purity of the English colonists), and only the English language was to be used. The fact that these statutes were deemed necessary is a strong indication of just how entrenched in Irish society the foreigners had become. Despite this and other attempts to tighten their grip on the island, English land shrank during the fifteenth century and would continue to diminish until the arrival of the English Tudor dynasty in the form of King Henry VIII.

### The Tudors and Stuarts

Henry reinforced English rule in Ireland. This was apparent in his ruthless dealings with any resistance fighters. One famous example is that of Thomas Fitzgerald of the Kildare clan, or "Silken" Thomas as he is more widely known. His resistance to English rule sent a clear message to Henry that to enforce and maintain his royal authority, he would need the house of Kildare. Never one to take threats lightly, Henry's response was unequivocal. He sent an army

### THEOBALD WOLF TONE

Born in 1763, Tone (1753–98) attended Trinity College, Dublin, where he studied law. He was an idealistic young Protestant who admired the French principles of liberty and equality, borne from the revolution. He became secretary of the Catholic Committee in 1792 and his abilities helped secure the right for Catholics to vote. He had also formed the secret Society of United Irishmen in Belfast in 1791. This group started as a debating society with its concentration on reform. However, when faced with overwhelming rejections on parliamentary reform and the liberation of Catholics, the society turned to more radical and violent means of change. Tone was sent to France to enlist the help of the new French Republic. He returned with an army to begin an Irish revolution. Misfortune hindered their efforts from the outset. Tone was unable to land at Bantry Bay and the Dublin militia, seeing the approaching army, began to disarm the United Irishmen. By the time Tone arrived the rebellion was already over. He was captured soon after landing in Ireland and sentenced to death. Before his sentence could be carried out, Tone committed suicide.

to crush any resistance—killing all those who surrendered and publicly executing Thomas Fitzgerald. After such a show of force and unswerving will the resistance movement weakened.

However, by far the most important change caused by Henry VIII—and still of the utmost relevance in today's Ireland—was his enforcement of the reformation of Ireland, changing its national religion from Catholicism to Protestantism. The religious reformation of Ireland began shortly after Henry's messy break from the Catholic Church. In 1536 Henry was named Supreme Head of the Church by the Irish Parliament, thus cementing his power in Ireland not only as monarch but also as spiritual leader. Despite some initial dissatisfaction about changes to the form of service, the people of Ireland—as in England—paid lip service to the reformation, perhaps due in no small part to the dissolution of the monasteries and the breakup of the Catholic Church's land and property. However, as was the case all over Europe at that time, the underlying religious issues continued simmering.

After some brief power struggles with the remaining Irish nobles, Henry VIII was officially declared King of Ireland in 1541. Henry's daughter, Elizabeth I, took the throne in 1558 following the death of her father and the comparatively short reigns of her protestant brother Edward VI (1547–1553) and her catholic sister Mary Tudor (1553–1558). Their time in power may have been short but it was marked by religious intolerance and executions.

Elizabeth fought passionately for the advancement of English rule in Ireland, both as monarch and religious leader. She was confirmed as head of the Irish church in 1560 and although by this point the persecution of the Protestants had abated somewhat, it is important to note that anger towards Protestantism became synonymous with unfair English treatment. Religion and politics combined once again and was indicative of what the future held for Ireland.

Elizabeth I was succeeded by the Scottish James VI, who became the first Stuart monarch of England as King James I. He soon introduced the Articles of Plantation. These new rules bought English and Scottish settlers over to Ireland where they were awarded land to farm—land that had previously belonged to the Irish. What little land the Irish landlords kept had to be farmed according to English practices. Inevitably such unfair treatment led once again to dissatisfaction, then rebellion. By the time the English Civil War started in 1642, this rebellion had seen the killing of many English settlers and an unsuccessful attack on Dublin. When the war ended with the execution of King Charles I, Ireland awaited England's response to their attacks. It was to come in the form of Oliver Cromwell.

### Ireland's Nemesis—Oliver Cromwell

Oliver Cromwell arrived in Ireland intent on squashing any uprising and restoring order to the country. The violence began in 1649. Cromwell attacked any remnants of Irish royalism, murdering entire gar-

risons when they refused to surrender and controlling all military activities. If you were Catholic or a royalist, you were not allowed to bear arms. Cromwell left Ireland in 1650, leaving Henry Ireton in his place as enforcer.

Ireton's mission did not end with the suppression of royalists. Another more insidious item on his agenda became apparent: the conversion—and if not that, then the oppression—of the entire Catholic population. The rights of Catholics were stripped away over the following decades. Land was taken and awarded to those seen to be more "loyal." Catholics were banned from Parliament, the legal professions, and governmental services, their church was banned by law, and they were not allowed to educate their children, either in Ireland or abroad. In the early part of the eighteenth century approximately three-quarters of the Irish population were Irish-Catholics, but they only owned about one-seventh of the land. Rebellion under these conditions was inevitable.

Theobald Wolfe Tone (see sidebar on page 15) was an idealistic young lawyer and secretary of the Catholic Committee that helped achieve the Catholic vote. In 1791 he founded the secret Society of United Irishmen and in the face of constant rejections in their fight for the rights of Catholics, they turned to revolutionary France and rebellion. In 1796 Tone set off from France with a large French army intent on revolution. The United Irishmen planned a national uprising for May 23, 1798, led by Lord Edward FitzGerald, son of the Duke of Leinster. However, the rebellion failed. Most of the society members were betrayed and arrested, and without leadership only uncoordinated, sporadic melees occurred, run by enthusiastic yet poorly armed peasants. Not even the arrival of Tone with French troops could save the day and Tone himself was captured and sentenced to death. The uprising did little to facilitate Catholic freedom and played into the hands of those politicians intent on unionization. The Act of Union was passed in 1800 and the Church of Ireland was joined to the Church of England.

Many visionaries followed in Tone's footsteps but with greater success. Pioneers such as Daniel O'Donnell fought and won equal rights for Catholics and the Irish in general. Yet ill feeling towards the English government remained, especially after its floundering reaction to the crippling potato famine from 1845 to 1851. Although the authorities did send aid, it was minimal and far from enough. It is estimated that Ireland lost two million of its inhabitants to starvation or emigration. Following this tragic episode, the Fenian movement was born.

Founded by James Stephens on St. Patrick's Day 1858, the Fenians were committed to an independent Ireland. They believed that change could only occur through the use of violence and began a campaign of bloodshed and rebellion. The idea of Irish independence, through the Home Rule Bill, was fought for by many influential men over the following years, but made slow progress. The eruption of World War I gave the British government an excuse to procrastinate on the issue and this gave rise to a small minority of republicans, including the Republican Brotherhood, making a dramatic bid for Irish freedom.

On Easter Monday 1916 an uprising broke out, mainly around the Dublin area of Ireland. The rebellion was stamped out by the authorities in less than a week since there was little public assistance for the republicans. But the British Government, engaged in a difficult war in Europe, reacted brutally to the captive leaders of the rebellion, executing 16 including injured James Connolly strapped to a chair. More than 2,000 people were interned, many on the mainland.

The uprising did not achieve its immediate aims—indeed, recent historians have debated its relevance to the cause of Irish independence—but in the longer term, the British reaction polarized feelings in Ireland. A little more than two years later a new force emerged in Irish politics. The Sinn Fein—meaning "We Ourselves"—movement swept through the polls and proclaimed itself the government for the whole of Ireland. Guerrilla warfare between Britain and Sinn Fein ensued and continued for many years. Eventually the British government amended the Home Rule Act so that the 26 counties of the Republic of Ireland would have complete independence but the remaining six counties of Northern Ireland would have to remain British—because their mainly Protestant population willed it so. This partitioning of the country was unpalatable to the nationalists and despite the bill being passed (by a tiny majority) civil war broke out, during which one of the great Irishmen of period, Michael Collins, was ambushed and killed by the Irish Republican Army. Peace finally came in 1923 when the republicans gave up their weapons. It was left to the ascetic Eamon de Valera to lead the Irish into nationhood.

Since World War II, partitioned Ireland has had a turbulent history. Nationalists pushed for a united Ireland and violence broke out again in the North in the 1970s when the vocal Catholic minority became a breeding ground for nationalist terrorists. The "Troubles" would see many deaths and little political progress until the end of the twentieth century, when it became obvious that international opinion had changed. The leaders of the IRA entered into talks with the British Government and, with a renunciation of violence in 2005, the door to a peaceful conclusion to the struggle seemed likely.

In the Republic, the last decades of the century saw the growth of a tiger economy. Fueled by the financial benefits of EU membership, the Republic surged into the twenty-first century revitalized and a significant player on the European stage. Tourism, which had struggled through the "Troubles," restarted: Dublin, Kerry, and the west coast becoming more accessible to visitors. Today, it is easier than ever before to discover Ireland's heritage.

## EAMON DE VALERA

Born in Brooklyn, New York City, in 1882 of Spanish-Irish parents, de Valera (1882–1975) was brought up in County Limerick where he became a schoolmaster, teaching math. He joined the Gaelic League and then the Irish Volunteers and led men in the Easter Rising in 1916. He was sentenced to be executed for his part in the rebellion and it was only the intervention of the U.S. consul that saw his sentence commuted to imprisonment. Released from jail in 1917, he campaigned against the conscription of Irish into the British Army and was jailed again, this time in Lincoln in England. In part the publicity of these events helped propel his Sinn Fein party into a huge electoral victory in 1918. He made a spectacular escape from prison and toured the United States, receiving funds and support that were used to great effect in the Anglo-Irish War that ended in the creation of the Republic. De Valera was opposed to partition, and boycotted the peace conference at which the treaty that divided Ireland was accepted. Marginalized during the Civil War, he formed the Fianna Fail party after the conflict and was swept to power in 1932. As Taoiseach (prime minister) he brought in a new constitution, managed to maintain neutrality in World War II in spite of pressure from Britain and the United States, and became President of the Republic in 1959, remaining in that position until he retired in 1973. He died two years later.

LEFT: Westport, Co. Mayo.

RIGHT: Ulster American Folk Park near Omagh, Co. Tyrone. This log farmhouse is a replica of a six-roomed dwelling built by Thomas Mellon and his father four years after their arrival in Pennsylvania.

**LEFT:** The picturesque parish church of Ballintoy with Rathlin Island behind. Some families still live on the island, which is almost treeless thanks to the fierce Atlantic gales.

**ABOVE:** Carrickfergus Castle in County Antrim, on the shore of Lough Belfast is one of the earliest stone castles in Ireland— if not the earliest. Building commenced during Henry II's reign (1154–89) as John de Courcy sought to hold onto the large tracts of Ulster he had conquered. Henry's son John (reigned 1199–1216) made it the center of government administration, a job it was to continue for many years.

**RIGHT:** The statue of protestant King William III in Carrickfergus.

**PAGE 20–21:** The ruined Franciscan Bonamargy Friary at Ballycastle was built by Rory MacQuillan in 1500.

**LEFT:** The Giant's Causeway, Ireland's only World Heritage Site, is a fantastic attraction—as is the whole of the "Causeway Coast." From Portrush to Ballycastle there are many places to hike and some extraordinary places—such as Dunluce Castle which features on the back cover of this book. This photograph of the causeway looks back to Aird's Snout, a promontory jutting out from the 400ft cliffs above.

**RIGHT:** East of the Giant's Causeway lies the sandy White Park Bay. One of the six counties that make up Northern Ireland, Antrim is situated in the northeast region of Ulster and it was here that Saint Patrick was enslaved for seven years before his escape back to Britain. Just a few miles away from the Giant's Causeway is the small village of Bushmills and it is here one can find the oldest (legal) whisky distillery in Ireland. Visitors to the distillery can take a tour, learn about the distilling processes and, of course, sample some of the product. Further along the Bushmills coastal road is Carrickarede—a small islet that is only linked to the mainland by a rope bridge. It is constructed every year by local fishermen and is now a famous phenomenon

**PAGE 26–27:**

**LEFT:** Another beautiful Atlantic beach. This is White Rocks Strand, near Portrush: further west is Portstewart Strand which is also protected by the National Trust. Portrush is famous for its world-class golf course.

**RIGHT:** Ballintoy is another pretty fishing village on the Antrim coast.

# County Armagh

PAGE 28–29: White Park Bay and the fishing village of Portbradden.

LEFT: Looking east over Coney Island on Lough Neagh, which is fortified with a motte and tower. The photograph was taken from the O'Connor stronghold on Derrywarragh Island at the mouth of the Blackwater River. Legend has it that Lough Neagh was created by the giant Finn MacCool. He picked up a chunk of ground and threw it into the Irish Sea—creating both the Isle of Man and the lough.

Often called "the Orchard of Ireland" due to the fruit growing country just north of the main city, County Armagh has a rich history and also boasts great beauty. For example, Apple Blossom Sunday in late May sees the hundreds of apple trees across the countryside burst into color as the blossoms of pink and yellow cover the trees as far as the eye can see. Named after the goddess Macha, Ard Macha (Macha's Height) the city of Armagh has an illustrious history. It was here the Saint Patrick founded his first church in A.D. 445. Despite the ravages of Viking attacks and English rule, Armagh has remained the spiritual capital of Ireland for the past 1,500 years. Saint Patrick's protestant cathedral now occupies the same spot previously occupied by Patrick's very first church, which had been built inside a hill fort. Saint Patrick's Catholic Cathedral also resides inside the city. It was completed in 1873 and originally designed by the architect J. T. Duff.

PAGE 32–33: The ancient monastic site of St. Mullins. The original monastery—which contains the burials of Celtic kings and kings of Leinster, was sacked by Vikings in A.D. 951 and was again burned in 1138. Most of the ruins visible today are from the abbey built on the site in the Middle Ages.

# County Carlow

**FAR LEFT:** Farmland near Kildavin.

**LEFT:** Carlow, the second smallest of all the Irish counties, is surrounded by the Barrow Valley and Killeshin Hills to the west and the picturesque Blackstairs Mountains to the East. Although it is believed that up to 150 castles were built here by the end of the fourteenth century by invading forces, none remain intact—although there are quite a few ruins that still impress. It is because of the many historic sites to be found here that Carlow has become known as the "Celtic Center of Ireland." One of the most impressive sights is the Browne Hill's Dolmen, a megalithic tomb dating back five thousand years. It is the burial site of a chieftain who was honored in death with a capstone that is the largest in Ireland., estimated to weigh 100 tons.

**BELOW:** The south wall of Ballymoon Castle dating to the thirteenth/early fourteenth centuries.

# County Cavan

A hugely popular area due to its varied landscapes and plentiful activities, both indoor and out, County Cavan is always worth a trip. Cavan's highest point is Cuilcach Mountain (2,188 feet) and it is here that the River Shannon, Ireland's longest river has its source. Most of the countryside is covered with low hills and lots of smaller lakes that have been created by the overflowing River Erne. Many of these lakes are incredibly picturesque and have outstanding fishing. This is Drumlane Church and round tower that lie by the River Erne, seven miles northwest of Cavantown near Milltown. One of St. Columba's monasteries, the medieval foundation dates to the thirteenth century. The church has carvings of bishops and abbots and other important figures.

# County Clare

St. Senan's cathedral church and round tower on
Scattery Island date back to A.D. 544. The monastery
felt the dread effect of the Vikings who fell on it in
A.D. 816, A.D. 835, and occupied it between A.D. 972
and 975. They were defeated by Brian Boru.

LEFT: The Cistercian Corcomroe Abbey was founded at the end of the twelfth century. This effigy in the choir is of Conor O'Brien who died in 1267.

ABOVE: Detail of the wonderful twelfth century Romanesque south door of the church at Dysert O'Dea. On the site of an early Christian monastery founded in the eighth century, the church was reconstructed in the seventeenth century. There is a round tower on the site dating to the same period.

RIGHT: The dramatic Cliffs of Moher run for five miles and reach 650ft.

**LEFT:** Quin Abbey had an interesting history. There was a church originally. It burned down in 1278 and in 1280 the Norman lord De Clare built a castle on the site. Some of this—parts of two massive towers—still remain, but it was destroyed by 1350 when another church was built there. The Franciscans arrived in 1433. It was desecrated by Cromwell's men in 1651 and the abbey had a checkered history after that, with periods of emptiness, and periods of occupation until the last friar to live there, John Hogan, died in 1820.

**ABOVE:** The cloisters—probably the best preserved Franciscan examples in Ireland.

**ABOVE:** Panel of MacMahon tomb built around 1475 in Ennis Friary. It shows Christ being laid in the tomb. Founded for the Franciscans around 1242, by the end of the fourteenth century there were 350 friars and a school of 600. It survived Henry VIII's Dissolution of the Monasteries thanks to the protection of the Earl of Thomond, but became a parish church in 1615. The friars had returned by the time Cromwell arrived, for his men killed many; they came back after the restoration of Charles II but the abbey was deserted by the end of the seventeenth century.

**RIGHT:** Poulnabrone prehistoric tomb on the limestone landscape of the Burren.

**FAR RIGHT:** Bunratty Castle, of mainly mid-fifteenth century construction, was restored in the 1950s.

**FAR LEFT:** Peat stooked for drying below Slievecallan west of Connolly. Bog covers some 15 percent of the Irish landscape—although this has been shrinking because of the use of peat for fertilizers and as a domestic fuel.

**LEFT:** Thatched cottage near Doolin.

**ABOVE:** Rain squall approaching the west coast of Co. Clare over the Aran Islands.

**PAGE 50–51:** O'Brien's Tower on top of the Cliffs of Moher was built by the Victorians as a viewing point.

County Cork

PAGE 52–53:
Cobh Harbor. Cobh—pronounced "cove"—is located on Great Island in Cork Harbor.

LEFT: Still considered by most southern Ireland residents to be the "real capital of Ireland," Cork is the largest of all counties and situated in the southwest corner of the country. Often playfully called "The Rebel Country" due to its history of taking a contrary stance against the rest of the country in important issues, West Cork is becoming an increasingly popular destination, not only for tourists but also for people looking to settle in Ireland. The natural, unspoiled, and rugged beauty of this area coupled with the extremely laid-back atmosphere that pervades every part of West Cork is a huge incentive to move here. In fact it is becoming an artisan heaven with, reportedly, a large number of musicians, actors, writers, and poets settling here. Cork City's Holy Trinity Church lies on South Channel of River Lee.

ABOVE RIGHT: Looking east along Cobh's sea front from the pier head.

RIGHT: The *Lusitania* monument in Cobh's freshly painted Casement Square.

LEFT: Kinsale Harbor from Charles Fort. West of Cork, Kinsale originated in Norman times, received its royal charter from Edward III in 1334, and was the site in 1601 of an attack by a Spanish fleet. They quickly took the town but were besieged by the English. Help came from Ulster in the form of Hugh O'Neill, whose Nine Years' War against the Tudors had started in 1594. He arrived in time to blockade the attackers. But the decisive battle in the war was betrayed and O'Neill's defiance ended in disaster. Kinsale was also the port at which James II arrived on March 12, 1689, and marched north to defeat on the Boyne. Kinsale fell to John Churchill and became an important English naval base well into the eighteenth century.

ABOVE: Youghal—pronounced "yawl"—is located on the coast to the east of Cork. At one time owned by Sir Walter Raleigh and later an English garrison town, the Clock Gate on Main Street dates from 1777. It once was the main gate to the city, then a prison.

PAGE 58–59: Cork has one of—if not the—most famous attractions in all of Ireland: the Blarney Stone. People have traveled for miles to hang upside down and kiss this stone in the hope of receiving the Irish "gift of the gab." The stone is found in Blarney Castle, which is one of the oldest in Ireland, having been built in 1446 as a stronghold for the Lords of Muskerry, the MacCarthy's. Blarney Castle has dramatic machiolations, in which the Blarney Stone is set. Machiolations are projecting parts of the parapet with holes in the floor—defenders used them to drop things on attackers.

BELOW LEFT: The landscape east of Knockboy and west of Conigar in the valley of Borlin looks toward the Shehy Mountains.

ABOVE LEFT: Bantry Bay. Looking across Glengarriff Harbor to the Caha Mountains.

RIGHT: Homeward bound to Baltimore Harbor with a backdrop of the southern cliffs of Sherkin Island. Baltimore was once attacked (on June 20, 1631) by Algerian pirates who carried off around a large number of people (the number varies in histories but seems to have been between 100 and 200). This event was immortalized by Thomas Osbourne Davis in the poem "The Sack of Baltimore."

# County Derry (or Londonderry)

PAGE 62–63 AND RIGHT: Two photographs that show the verdant lushness of the Emerald Isle—they show the Roe Valley landscape south of Dungiven in Co. Derry. Known as Derry by nationalists and Londonderry by Unionists, this county is one of the six that make up Northern Ireland. County Derry was created when the former County Coleraine was combined with various small parts of Antrim, Donegal, and Tyrone. This was done at the specific request of London companies so they would have unrestricted control of the mouths of rivers Bann and Foyle, thus ensuring themselves enough wood for building. Derry has many interesting places and stories; in fact it was in the Derry town of Limavady that Miss Jane Ross acquired the tune of "Danny Boy" from a traveling fiddler. Also, in 1932 the famous pilot Amelia Earhart landed her plane on a hill in the town of Ballyarnet, where to this day there is a center dedicated to the intrepid American flyer.

BELOW: "Roaring Meg" is an eighteen-pounder of 1642 that was used in the defense of the city against the forces of James II. Today it can be seen on the walls overlooking the Bogside below.

RIGHT: Dungiven Priory was founded by Augustinians in 1100. This is reputed to be the tomb of Cooey-na-Gal ("terror of the stranger") O'Cahan who died in 1385. The panel below is of six armed soldiers wearing kilts.

# County Donegal

Not part of Northern Ireland but still in the province of Ulster, Donegal contains mainly low mountains and loughs (lakes), including Lough Swilly and Lough Derg. There are also two inhabited islands off the coast of Donegal, Arranmore and Tory Island. The weather here tends to be mild since it is influenced by the Gulf Stream, so winters are wet but not too cold, and summers are cool and damp. This is Portsalon beach on the Fanad peninsula, across Lough Swilly from Inishowen.

LEFT: In the south of Co. Donegal, west of Ardara, lie the steep sea cliffs of Slieve League (see pages 68–69). Round the coast is Donegal Bay. This photograph shows the lighthouse at St. John's Point near Killybegs Harbor.

ABOVE LEFT: Malin Head is the most northerly point of Ireland, sited on Donegal's Inishowen Peninsula. This photograph shows the view looking southeast from Malin Head across White Strand Bay into Inishowen.

ABOVE: The Neolithic Kilclooney Dolmen (portal tomb) near Ardara has a capstone that is 13ft long and 20ft wide. This and its partner are all that remain of a cairn that was nearly 100ft long

Page 76–77: Tory Island off Horn Head, west of the Fanad Peninsula.

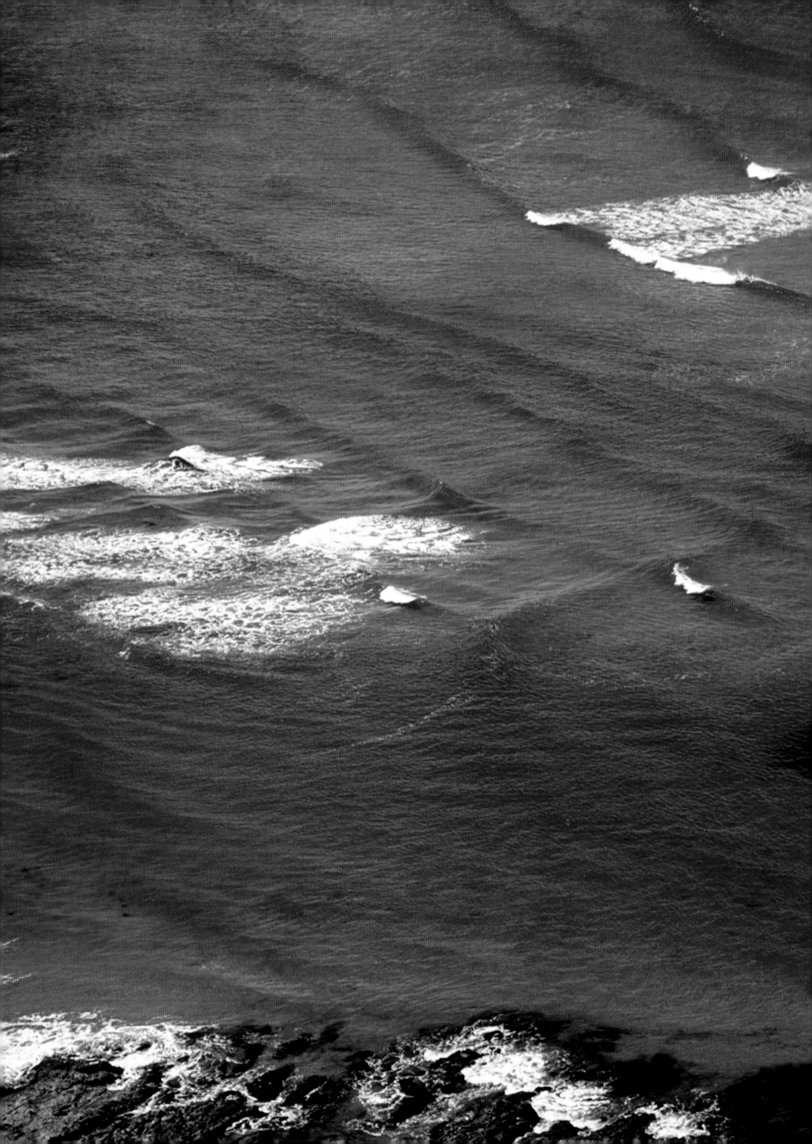

# County Down

Ireland has many beauties to offer, both geological and
architectural, yet no county combines them so neatly as
County Down. Travelers can find many treats here that
in other counties they would need to travel miles
to find. Beautiful beaches, saltwater and freshwater
fishing, boating, bird-watching, two excellent forests,
castles, gardens, horse riding, and the world-famous
Royal County Down Golf Course are all on hand.
Photograph shows Scrabo Tower on Scrabo Hill,
Newtownards at head of Strangford Lough, was built
in 1857 as a memorial to the third Marquis of
Londonderry.

THIS PICTURE: Legananny Dolmen near Castlewellan is another important Neolithic site in Co. Down. Some 5,000 years old, it is known locally as "the giant's grave."

FAR RIGHT: The lightship restaurant at Sketrick Island on the west shore of Strangford Lough, a few miles from Belfast.

THIS PICTURE: As of January 1994, the county of Dublin officially ceased to exist because the government decided that, being the most centralized country in the entire of the European Union, it was undemocratic from a local government standpoint. County Dublin was disposed of and replaced with the separate counties of Dun Laoghaire-Rathdown, Fingal, and South Dublin. Starting in 2006 all official maps will no longer say "County Dublin," but will list the new separate counties instead. Officially the entire area will be referred to as the "Dublin Region." This is Dublin Castle, that was started in the thirteenth century, although the round tower is as late as the seventeenth century.

PAGE 84–85: Christchurch Cathedral was founded in 1038 by Dunan, the first Bishop of Dublin. Dublin was taken by the Normans in the shape of Richard de Clare, Earl of Pembroke—Strongbow—whose tomb this is said to be. (It isn't; it dates to around 1340 and was moved here from a church in Drogheda.)

# County Fermanagh

Enniskillen itself possesses many interesting sights, including Enniskillen Castle, Castle Coole, and—shown here—Old Crom Castle on the shore of Upper Lough Erne. A plantation castle of around 1611, it burned down in the eighteenth century.

**ABOVE:** Lower Lough Erne is a beautiful area with many historical sites. Of particular interest are the religious foundations set up on the islands—the monastery on White Island has a row of pagan figures set into a wall. Pictured here on Boa Island is one of two ancient pagan carved heads now in Caldragh graveyard. They are pre-Christian Celtic

**RIGHT:** Fermanagh is famous for fishing. The Erne is famous for its winter pike and roach fishing and Lough Melvin offers spring salmon and many different kinds of trout. This a photograph shows the landscape on the edge of Lower Lough Erne, two miles north of Enniskillen.

**PAGE 92–93:** At the southern end of Lower Loch Erne, on the River Erne, stands Enniskillen Castle. Originally built 600 years ago by the Maguires, it was destroyed in 1602 and rebuilt as a plantation castle. Strategically placed, it became a garrison fort and a military barracks. Today it houses the museum of one of the great Irish regiments: the Royal Inniskilling Fusiliers.

LEFT AND BELOW LEFT: Two views of the priory, round tower, and church ruins on Devenish Island, Lower Lough Erne. It was St. Molaise who set up the monastery here in the sixth century. As with so many sites in Ireland it was raided and burned by the Vikings, but it had a long history, remaining in use until the seventeenth century. The round tower—a fantastic example some 82 feet tall—is well preserved. The highest point on the island is dominated by St. Mary's Priory, a fifteenth century Augustinian church.

BELOW: Monea Castle is another seventeenth century plantation castle. It was badly damaged in the Confederate War of 1642–53. This was that part of the English Civil War that saw Royalists and Roundheads fighting in Ireland. It started with Royalist victories and ended with Cromwell's subjugation of Ireland. Monea was finally abandoned in the eighteenth century.

Kilronan town on Inishmore, the largest town on the
Aran Islands.

**FAR LEFT:** The Aran Islands—view across Trawmore at the south end of Inishmore toward Straw Island lighthouse. The three Aran Islands—Inishmore, Inishmaan, and Inisheer—sit in Galway Bay. They are much-visited by tourists with attractions such as Dun Aonghasa Iron Age fort, the Seven Churches monastic settlement, and Kilronan—the main port.

**LEFT:** Landscape four miles southeast of Leenaun in an area of Connemara known as "Joyce country." This is in the Maumturk mountains, whose highest point is Mount Twelve Pins (2,395ft).Now an unspoiled and tranquil land with an increasingly thriving capital, Co. Galway has suffered its fair share of misfortune. It was invaded by the Normans in the late twelfth century, ruled by warring Anglo-Normans, and witnessed one of the bloodiest battles in the history of Ireland—the Battle of Aughrim. Williamite and Jacobite armies met on the July 12, 1691. The Williamites won the battle, but at the cost of an estimated 9,000 lives. Like much of Ireland, Galway suffered greatly in the 1845 potato famine, with much of the population either dying from hunger or emigrating to America.

**PAGE 100–101:** Cromwell's Castle on the island of Inishbofin—the "island of the white cow" off Galway's west coast. Another lonely island chosen for a monastic settlement, the main harbor was defended by a castle that was occupied by a Spanish pirate in the sixteenth century. It was captured by Cromwell in 1653 and his forces used it as a prison for catholic priests.

PAGE 102–103: Clonfert Cathedral is small, old—the monastic site it occupies was founded in A.D. 563 by St. Brendan—and a wonderful example of Romanesque architecture and decoration. This photograph shows a detail of the Romanesque doorway, which dates to the twelfth century.

THIS PICTURE: O'Brien Castle on Inisheer, the smallest of the Aran Islands.

PAGE 106–107: Another view of the island of Inishbofin. This shows the *Lady of Lourdes* wreck and East Village.

**RIGHT:** Fiddaun Castle, a sixteenth century tower built and owned by the O'Shaughnessy family. They lived in it until 1574, and owned it until it was confiscated in 1697.

**BELOW RIGHT:** Photograph of a Galway Bay "hooker" at Kinvara on Galway Bay. These sailing craft in Galway Bay and around the Connemara coast supported a significant fishing industry in the nineteenth century.

**OPPOSITE, ABOVE:** Dongary Castle in the village of Kinvara. A small sixteenth century castle, Dongary was built on an earlier sixth century site, the seat of King Guaire Aidhneach of Connacht.

**OPPOSITE, BELOW:** Looking east across Inishlyon toward the mainland coast.

**PAGE 110–111:** Wreck of the cargo ship *Plassy* on the east shore of Inisheer. South Island Lighthouse is in the distance.

# County Kerry

**LEFT:** Looking southwest from Dunmore Head to the islands of Great Blasket, Inishnabro, and Inishvickillane.

**ABOVE:** The view south from Bray Head on Valentia Island along the cliffs by Dromgour, part of the Ring of Kerry. The ring is a route around the Iveagh Peninsula that takes in mountain and coastal scenery—Macgillicuddy's Reeks, the Lakes of Killarney, and Staigue Fort (see photo at right).

**RIGHT:** Staigue stone fort is on the south of the Iveagh Peninsula. It probably dates to the early Iron Age and is a fine example of early stone forts with walls up to 18ft high and 13ft thick. Some reconstruction took place in the nineteenth century, but this has not destroyed the site's interest or value.

**PAGE 114–115:** Sea squall over the Blasketts. The islands lie off Dunmore Head at the southwest tip of the Dingle Peninsula. The main islands are Great Blasket, Inishtooskert, Inishnabro, and Inishvickillane.

**RIGHT:** Known to the Irish as "The Kingdom," County Kerry, like its neighbor Cork, is bordered by the River Shannon and the Atlantic Ocean. The countryside of Kerry is full of mountains, ruins, remote villages, and bustling towns.
The coast of Kerry boasts large peninsulas—this is St. Finian's Head—and bays including The Dingle Peninsula and the "Ring of Kerry," which offers a popular cycle path for the more adventurous (and energetic) explorers. Kerry also has Ireland's highest mountains—the Macgillicuddy's Reeks—two national parks and perhaps the most famous town in Ireland, Killarney.

**PAGE 118:** Caherciveen is the largest town in the Ring of Kerry. It is known for three things: the remarkable number of pubs; the only catholic church not dedicated to a saint or to God—it's dedicated to Daniel O'Connell (see page 11); and "Monks going to Skelligs" by sculptor Eamon O'Doherty.

**PAGE 119:** Valentia Island is linked to the mainland by a causeway to Portmagee. It's also close to the Skellig Islands, which lie about 10 miles off the Iveagh Peninsula. Valentia houses the Skellig Experience Center which tells about the monastery on Skellig Michael and what it was like to live in such conditions. This photograph was taken looking across the lighthouse on Fort Point over Beginish Island toward Mt. Knocknadeba.

**PAGE 120–121:** Early Christian cell on Church Island on the edge of Beginish Island near Caherciveen.

# County Kildare

LEFT: St. Brigid's Well, south of Kildare Town, is reputed to have healing powers. It is located near the Black Abbey where tradition has it that St. Brigid founded a famous monastery in the fifth or sixth centuries A.D.

RIGHT AND PAGE 124–125: Two details of the Moone Cross showing (RIGHT) intertwined animals, and (PAGE 124–125) a detail of the east face showing Abraham sacrificing Isaac. The Moone Cross is 17ft high and stands in the grounds of an early Christian monastery that is said to have been founded by St. Columba.

BELOW: Horses and donkeys graze on the edge of the Bog of Allen near Rathangan. The largest bog in Ireland—it is an area of around 370 square miles between the Liffey and Shannon rivers, the peat is commercially harvested and used in power stations.

123

# County Kilkenny

Kilree High Cross and Round Tower near Dunnamag-
gan. The tower is 96ft high and the cross, possibly ninth
century in origin, is a fine  example of geometric motifs.

**LEFT:** Farmland just north of the village of Kells, Co. Kilkenny. Kilkenny comprises the ideal mix of old and new. The capital of Kilkenny, often called "The Marble City," has many well-preserved medieval buildings alongside some of the best nightlife in the world. The annual comedy festival has earned worldwide recognition as one of the best in Europe, and Kilkenny also accommodates Ireland's oldest arts festival.

**ABOVE:** Jerpoint Abbey is one of the most impressive ruins in Ireland. A Cistercian house founded in 1158, it became affiliated with another great Cistercian foundation—Fountains Abbey in Yorkshire—in 1227. The cloistered quadrangle is particularly evocative and it is from the cloister pillars that this detail of a bishop and a knight is taken.

With its towers and curtain wall, Kells Priory looks more like a castle than a religious foundation. It has sat on the banks of the King's River since 1193 when Geoffrey FitzRobert—Strongbow's brother-in-law—brought five canons to Ireland from Cornwall. It needed the walls as it was attacked three times in the fourteenth century, in 1326 by the Scottish army of Robert Bruce's brother Edward. Its fate was the fate of so many such monasteries: it was dissolved in 1540 and became the property of the Earl of Ormonde.

# County Laois

LEFT: Laois is one of the twelve landlocked Irish counties. Mostly flat, this is the Rock of Dunamase, situated just outside the town of Stradbally. This 150-foot-high rock outcropping is capped with the demolished ruins of a complex fortress dating back to 1497.

THIS PICTURE: Lea Castle near Portarlington.

# County Limerick

Full of undulating low-lying land, Limerick is part of the
country known as "The Golden Vale." This photograph
shows Anhid ancient cemetery a little south of the
village of Croom.

THIS PICTURE: Adare Castle lies on the River Maigue. It was a grand building with a great hall along the river frontage and a stone keep on the site of an older ringfort. The castle was slighted at the end of the sixteenth century and again by Cromwell.

PAGES 140–141:
LEFT: Landscape near Granard, a small market town that was sacked by Edward Bruce in 1315.

RIGHT: Façade of St. Mel's Cathedral, a nineteenth century grey limestone building—on a site said to have been founded by St. Mel in the fifth century. Certainly there was an earlier site: excavations in the 1960s showed traces of eighth century timbers.

# County Longford

# County Louth

Situated on the east coast of Ireland, Louth is often referred to as the little county or "the wee county." It is believed that this is because it was once the smallest of the original counties and named "An Lu" in Irish (meaning "the least"). However this is not the case; the county actually gets its name from the small village of Louth, which was named after the Celtic god Lugh. This is the view east across the Moyry Pass from Old Faughart Church.

# County Mayo

Mayo is a county of stark contrasts. The north
boasts islands, bog lands, estuaries and sharp
peninsulas. The South is mainly lush and serene
farmland. It is both an inspiring and challenging
place with many historically important sights
worth seeing. This is the view across Killany
harbor from Leenaun to the Mweelrea
Mountains—from Co. Galway to Co. Mayo.

LEFT: Stone carving inside Fourknocks prehistoric tomb.

BELOW: Prehistoric field boundaries and the pyramidal interpretation Center at the Ceide Fields. These fields are the oldest known systems in the world—over 5,500 years old. This unique Neolithic landscape has been preserved in peat bog.

**RIGHT:** Aerial view of a rath—a circular earthen fortress sometimes outlined by rocks—five miles south of Ballina, a busy market town on the estuary of the River Moy.

**PAGE 150–151:** Travelers to Mayo should not leave without taking in the breathtaking sight of Achill Island, in particular Grainne Ni Mhaille's Tower in Kildavnet—the tower of the fearless pirate queen. The island also boasts wonderful beaches, deep sea fishing, and boating. This picture postcard place is both striking and tranquil and well worth visiting. This view of Achill looks northwest across Ashleam Bay toward Dooega.

Mayo has had many famous inhabitants in its history. A few of the more famous ones were Sir Robert Peel, the founder of the British police force and the more infamous than famous Captain Charles Boycott whose main contribution was the addition of his name to the dictionary. He was such a cruel landlord that his tenants refused to work for him as a protest against his awful treatment—a boycott. Fans of the John Wayne movie The Quiet Man may appreciate a visit to the innovative "Quiet Man Heritage Cottage" in Cong. This novel museum treats its visitors to a complete quiet man experience while at the same time exhibiting many archaeological and historical items.

# County Meath

Trim Castle on the River Boyne. Steeped in history and containing some of the most impressive Neolithic monuments in all of Ireland, Meath is a county like no other. Once known as "The Royal County," it was home for the High Kings of Ireland and it was here, on the famous hill at Tara, where kings were crowned. Many of Ireland's most important prehistoric sites are located in Meath. The landscape is mainly rich grazing land streaked by the winding rivers of Boyne and Blackwater. These two rivers meet at Navan and stretch on to the Irish Sea. The legend of the River Boyne, Fionn MacCumhall, and the Salmon of Knowledge is still told throughout the land, even today. The rivers are brimming over with salmon and trout, a treat for any eager angler.

**LEFT AND ABOVE:** The Boyne Valley is scattered with countless megalithic tombs and passage graves, including the famous structures at Dowth, Knowth, Loughcre, and Newgrange—quite simply one of the iconic passage tombs of Western civilization. The huge barrow is 280ft in diameter by 40ft high and covers one of the finest passage graves in Europe. Built around 3200 B.C., Newgrange is aligned with the winter solstice, and has a corbeled ceiling which reaches a height of 20ft above the floor.

# County Monagahan

Clones round tower is around 75ft tall. The monastery was founded by St. Tighernach in the sixth century.

# County Offaly

LEFT: Clonony Castle near Cloghan is a sixteenth century, four-storied tower house.

RIGHT: The Nun's Church at Clonmacnois was completed in 1166. The monastery was founded in A.D. 548–549 by St. Ciaran.

# County Roscommon

**LEFT:** The famous poet W.B. Yeats spent his youth in the Isle of Innisfree in Lough Gill, next to the county town of Sligo, and claimed much of his inspiration came from the surrounding landscapes. He died in 1939 and his grave can be found in Drumcliffe.

*"I will arise and go now, and go to*
*Innisfree,*
*And a small cabin build there, of clay*
*and wattles made;*
*Nine bean rows will I have there, a*
*hive for the honey bee,*
*And live alone in the bee-loud glade."*

**FAR LEFT:** Looking east over Lough Key with willowherb in foreground.

**ABOVE:** The Cistercian Boyle Abbey was set up in 1161 and most of it was built in the twelfth and thirteenth centuries. The most important abbey in Connacht, it was severely treated by Cromwell's men in 1659.

# County Sligo

Sligo is found on the western side of Ireland, right next door to
County Mayo and County Roscommon. The Irish name Sligeach
actually means "place of many shells." The county earned this name
due to the profusion of shellfish found in the nearby River Gar-
avogue. It is recorded in Ordnance Survey letters in 1836 that cart-
loads of shells were found under the ground as more houses were
being built and more earth was turned. Visitors to Sligo can enjoy a
boat ride from the town into Lough Gill, which offers one of the
most romantic views of all the Irish lakes.

# County Tipperary

Immortalized in the World War I song "It's a long way to Tipperary," this county has many notable places to visit and gorgeous vistas to admire, such as this example of the landscape of Co. Tipperary: looking north to Caher from Sugarloaf Hill.

PAGE 166–167 AND RIGHT: Perhaps the foremost site in Tipperary is the Rock of Cashel. Dominating the landscape for many miles, the Rock is less then a quarter of a mile wide and rises erect from the flat plains that surround it. The Rock is crowned with many medieval ruins, including a chapel (detail RIGHT), a round tower, and a cathedral. Many legends surround this place. It is said that Saint Patrick explained the workings of the Holy Trinity using a cloverleaf on this spot. It is also claimed that the rock was spit out by the Devil when he took a bite out of the nearby mountain now known as "Devil's Bit."

FAR RIGHT: Looking northwest over Clogheen to the Galty Mountains from Sugarloaf Hill.

BELOW: Romanesque arch in Cormac's Chapel which was built 1127–34. The Rock was a major seat of power until the siege by Cromwell led to 3,000 casualties.

County Tyrone

**LEFT:** Perhaps the foremost site in Tipperary is the Just outside the county town of Omagh at Camphill is the Ulster-American Folk Park. Concentrating on the theme of emigration, the park has grown up around the

boyhood home of Thomas Mellon and compares what he left (forge, school, church) to what he emigrated to in the United States (log cabin, barn, smokehouse). Thomas Mellon was a huge emigration success story. He left Ireland when he was five and became a judge, a banker, and eventually a millionaire. This nineteenth century log house (seen in the Ulster American Folk Park) was originally built on the Coz family farm, Greene County, Pennsylvania by Uriah Heep.

**PAGE 172–173:** One of the least-populated counties in Northern Ireland, Tyrone is a lush yet arresting place. What it lacks in people in more than makes up for in fascinating Celtic and prehistoric ruins—such as Beaghmore prehistoric stone circles 10 miles northwest of Cookstown.

# County Waterford

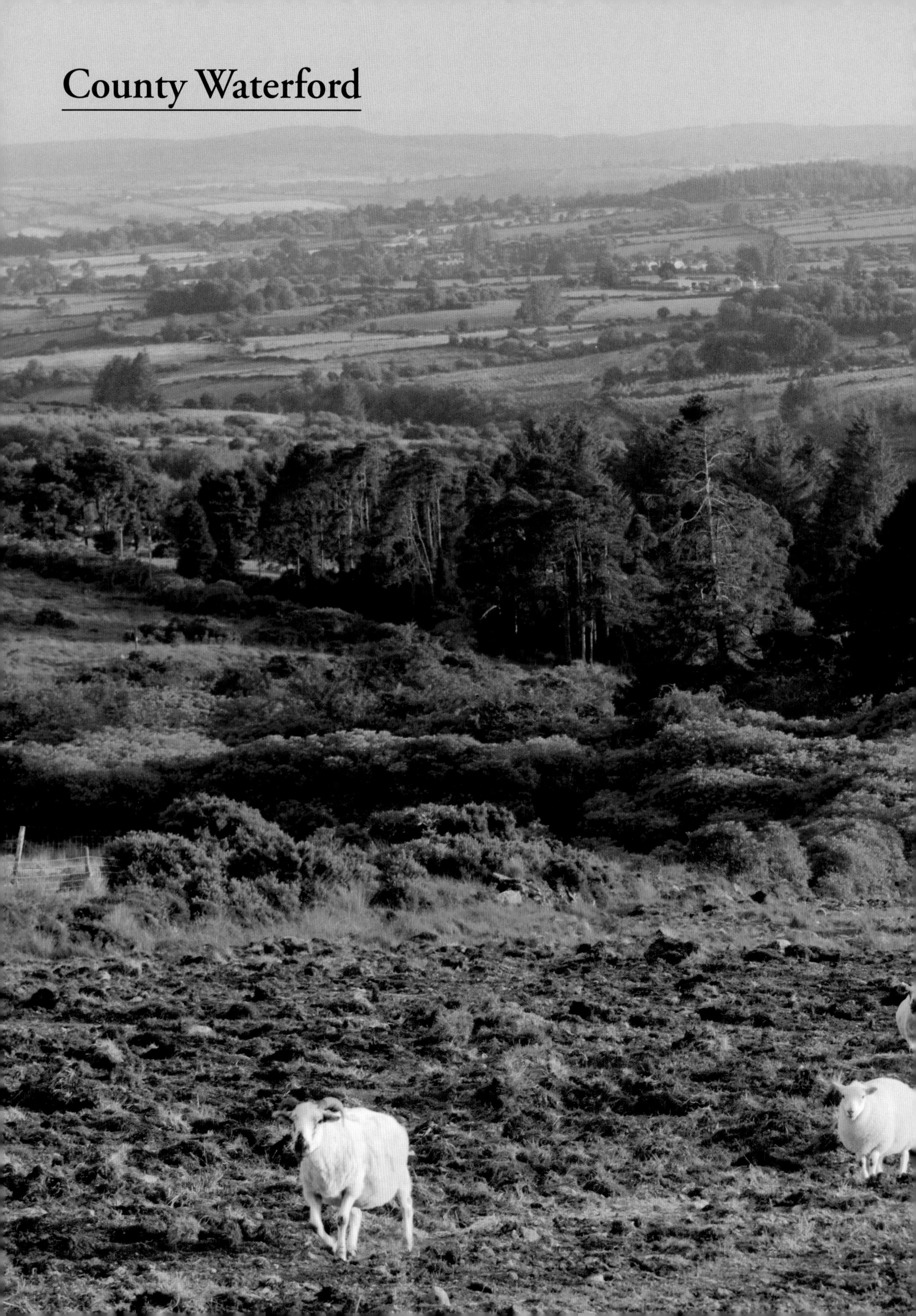

PAGE 174–175: View south from the Knockmealdown Mountains to the Blackwater Valley.

LEFT: Ardmore Church and round tower showing Romanesque panels on the exterior west wall.

RIGHT: Meadows on the banks of the River Blackwater near Cappoquin.

# County Westmeath

The remains of the thirteenth century Benedictine
Fore Priory, dedicated to St. Feichín and St. Taurin.
Confiscated by the English during the Hundred Years
War, it was fortified in the fifteenth century—although
this did not stop supression at the time of the
Dissolution of the Monasteries.

THIS PICTURE: The Hill of Ushnagh—one of several earthworks and stone structures on this ancient site. Said to be a meeting-place each May Day for the men of Ireland, the nearby "Catstone" (so named because it looks like a cat stalking a mouse) stands in the mythic center of Ireland, where the five provinces converge.

RIGHT: Near the important monastic site of Fore Priory is the very unusual .Anchorite's Cell, with its square tower. Anchorites were men or women who were enclosed for life in a cell, giving their time up to prayer and contemplation. The most famous occupant of this cell was Patrick Beglan during the seventeenth century.

# County Wexford

Hook Head lighthouse is one of the oldest operational lighthouses in the world. There has been a light here since the sixth century. The current building is medieval. Dating from 1172, apart from a short closure in the seventeenth century, it has been operational for 800 years—manned until it was automated in 1996.

THIS PICTURE: Replica of the immigrant ship *Dunbrody* on the quayside at New Ross. The original ship was built in Quebec in 1845 and she worked in the Atlantic until 1870.

RIGHT: Ballyhack castle and harbor. The castle dates back to the fifteenth or sixteenth century, strategically sited on the Waterford estuary.

# County Wicklow

Known as "The Garden of Ireland," County Wicklow is found on the eastern coast of Ireland, just south of County Dublin—in fact it is still considered to be part of the greater Dublin area. This beautiful countryside is northwest of Laragh in the Wicklow Mountains, just below the Wicklow Gap.

The round tower at Glendalough—a monastic settlement founded by St. Kevin in the sixth century An important site that is often refered to in the Irish annals, it was taken by the Normans and added to the See of Dublin. The round tower is 100ft tall with a conical roof that was rebuilt in the nineteenth century.

LEFT: St. Kevin's Church—also known as St. Kevin's kitchen—at Glendalough has a small round tower above the west doorway.

THIS PICTURE: Landscape in the Wicklow Mountains south of the Sally Gap.

PAGE 192: Interior of living room in Melton Homestead. Ulster American Folk Park near Omagh, Co. Tyrone.